Praise
At Rest

"'Make it true.' These words from the introductory poem 'Linea Nigra' are the earth and soul of William Jolliff's bountiful new collection *At Rest in My Father's House*. In the raw, real light of Jolliff's memory we are drawn to his deep sense of empathy for and identification with the hardscrabble farming families of his rural Ohio homeland, folks ever at the mercy of the weather and market's whims. These forces and the values shared in community shape them into tragic figures like Merle Freeman who lost everything and his life, or tender, like old Tilly with her 'patched dress' and 'mothering hand' who 'wrote down words to songs she'd sung forever.' Of all the unforgettable stories, told seamlessly by a poet sure of his voice and his craft, it is Jolliff's portrayal of his father that held me hardest. The son's struggle to understand his harsh, unyielding father for whom truck and tractor were life, is relieved by his reach for grace, grace we encounter in a poem like 'Suppertime': 'I can see him / now, leaning on his left arm, eating with the right / his talk fading into a picture I carry here. Right here.'"

—Suzanne Underwood Rhodes, Poet Laureate of Arkansas,
author of *Flying Yellow*

"These poems glean grace from the abandoned fields and towns of a Midwest childhood that led, eventually, to an academic life. God and banjos, family and loss weave through these rich pages. The well-rung lines narrate vivid vignettes, and then each poem turns, and its meaning leaps beyond the immediate confines of its purported subject. The result is verse that sings, that bites, that haunts."

—Jeffrey Bilbro, editor in chief, *Front Porch Republic*

"I don't know of any other poet who tills the dark soil of memory's hard geography as deeply and beautifully as Bill Jolliff. In the manner of Ron Rash or Mary Oliver, Jolliff attends to what others might deem unworthy of notice or ordinary. Through the powers of his keen ear, eye, and finely honed lyric, Jolliff makes the small and insignificant necessary and extraordinary. Each poem bristles with fierce energy. Each poem jolts me to a state of utter wonder and awe."

—Gina Ochsner, winner of the Flannery O'Connor, Raymond Carver and Kurt Vonnegut Awards for fiction, author of *The Hidden Letters of Velta B*

"Bill's poems come with a mule's epiphanic kick, breathing histories of lived life in rural Ohio that prove to be accessible and revelatory. Here the comic sits beside or within the tragic— these poems bring to mind Edgar Lee Masters, Wendell Berry, and Maurice Manning. They carry the regional authenticity of diction, a syntactical, sonic and rhetorical grit, and hold an intergenerational tension having to do with a disappearing or already disappeared way of life: family farms transformed and subsumed by agribusiness. If you wish to understand the rural half of America, you must read this!"

—Dave Mehler, author of *Roadworthy*, editor of *Triggerfish Critical Review*

"By day, William Jolliff is a college professor in Western Oregon; by night he remains a chore-bound farm boy in Southern Ohio. It is this deeply soiled and dieseled version of the poet that so eloquently inhabits the difficult beauties of the place and people he is from. *At Rest in My Father's House* is almost anything but that. But his sweat-soaked, banjo-stricken lines remind me, again and again, of that ancient dictum from the Scriptures: 'Strive to enter into rest.'"

—Paul J. Willis, author of *Somewhere to Follow*

"The poems in Jolliff's newest collection are saturated with exquisite detail and imagery, unforgettable characters, and dry wit. Reading these poems is akin to reading a collection of interrelated short stories grounded in the rural and the particular. I am confident readers will be grateful for the journey into the lives of people wrestling with death, loss, and hope."

—Nathaniel Lee Hansen, editor of *The Windhover*

At Rest in My Father's House

poems

William Jolliff

Aubade Publishing
Ashburn, VA

Edited by Joe Puckett

Cover design and book layout by Cosette Puckett

Library of Congress Control Number: 2022933510

ISBN: 978-1-951547-21-9

Published by Aubade Publishing, Ashburn, VA

Printed in the United States of America

For Aunt Lindy and Uncle John,
who took me to my first poetry reading

Remember the days of old,
　　consider the years of many generations:
ask thy father, and he will shew thee;
　　thy elders, and they will tell thee.

—Deuteronomy 32:7

Contents

Proem   1
Linea Nigra   3

Part I   5
The Barns   6
Coming to Know My Fathers   8
Calf-Mix Cups   10
Driving with My Father   11
The Gleaners   12
Cleaning Seed   13
John Deere Green   14
Brogans   15
Winter Plowing   16
All Good Things   17
The Way My Father Farmed   18
Suppertime   19
The Grip   20
Where Is My Father Now?   21
The End of the Homeplace   22

Part II   23
Cards on the Farm   24
Merle Freeman's Auction   26
First Snow   27
The Season of Heaven   29
In Praise of Cowards   30
Miss Tuttle's Sixth Grade, Fulton Elementary   31
Buzzards Wheeling   32
A Boy and His Dog   33
The War in Ohio   34
The Man Who Shoots Stop Signs   36
What He Needed   37
Milking in the Dark   39
Farm Widow   41
Explanations for the Night   42
The Blue Plate   43

Part III   **45**

The Old Ways   46
Songs We Live By   47
Patch's Wife   48
His Last House   50
The Woman with the Wooden Arm   51
Brother Everest Cleans His .22s   52
Collector Glass   53
What Tilly Knew   54
Hanover Lindy and the Miracle   55
Walter Mack, Reloading   57
Uncle Walt's Shoulders   58
The Duty of Crows   60

Part IV   **61**

The Lovely Miss McKendry, School Librarian   62
Scholarship Boy   64
The Farmer and the Silent *S*   66
The Language You Were Born To   68
Yes, All of It   69
The Professor Who Loved Banjos   70
Having Mastered Time Travel, Mark Twain Visits the
    Walmart Supercenter   71
Whittier at Midnight   72
A Quiet Place to Pray   73
Advice for a Dipshit Colleague Who Should Know   74
Vancouver Woman Beats Her Husband to Death with a Hammer   75
Why We Keep Teaching   77
Making Bread, Making Do   78
Mourning Ritual   80
On God's Tooth   81
Waiting for the Specialist, I Dream of Fulton Creek   82
Still Life with Banjo   83

Coda   **85**

At Rest in My Father's House   87

At Rest in My Father's House

Proem

Linea Nigra

*In certain civilizations . . . the earth was
considered as mother and you weren't allowed
to hurt her in any way with hard tools.
That was a rule.*

—Jacques Ellul

Before you sink that first share in a field
of stubble or stalks, afire with the light
of a bright November morning, idle down
your diesel. That smokestack is a candle,
and its sharp carbon scent—that's your prayer.

Now plow on. Mark off the headland as straight
as you can. Sight it in steady against
a tree or fence post. Never let your eye
wander. The way you pray the furrow
is the way you'll turn the field. Make it true.

There's a lushness in that new groove that's more
than just a wrinkle, more than a moist lip
of brown. You could almost call it a vein,
but it's more than that, too. Let it speak to you.
Let it say, *This is where we all begin.*

Part I

The Barns

Long before I was born
the glory left the barns,
the clear-purposed tackle
and singular fixtures
of a thousand daily tasks,

pens perfected in the shape
of life and turning seasons,
the brooding room for hens,
the farrowing pens for swine,
the stalls for bucket calves,

the loading shoots, gone,
the tackle rack, gone,
the pegs for hoes and spades,
for rope and wire, gone,
buggy whips and lanterns, gone—

they'd all gone back to dust,
those lost designs, the work
of brilliant, long-dead hands
all dissolved in the cool dark,
into close and tombish air,

into dust that only faintly kept
the memory of hens and hogs,
the chaffy dung of sweaty teams
that gnawed the gates for salt,
the powdery dirt of intention.

My years were diesel years,
the detritus of snapped tools,
crackled belts with worn cords,
plate steel and tinkered chain,
dual clamps, split wheels,

post-setters and fence-stretchers,
tractor parts and grease and anger
at the faces in the radio,
telling tales of too much rain
and the markets always down.

What was leaving and left
were the offal of debt,
of mechanical desperation—
the barn itself not worth saving,
save as we try to hold it here.

Coming to Know My Fathers

A midnight stillness filled Grandpa's shop
even by day. He was a carpenter,
and he kept his tools as closely as
he kept his own counsel. Some days
if she was sure he'd be gone on a job,
my grandmother would let me in.
The gravel floor was raked clean.
Axes, brooms, edgers, picks,
posthole diggers, scythes, shovels,
and spades sang the alphabet song
along the west and north ends.
Lumber was stacked along the east,
but the south was the holy of holies:
his workbench. It whispered secrets
of order and time. Sets of chisels
arranged in quarter-inch increments,
fifteen different files, candy counters
of wrenches and drill bits, all at hand.

Even then it seemed to me strange kin
to the back shed on my father's farm,
where crooked makeshift benches cut
from knotty, rough-sawn two-by-eights
were stained with oil and grease, heaped
with just the vaguest sense of what
the hell went where, and the dirt floor
was strewn with whatever dropped.
There, an ancient welder and drill press

fought for space with oil cans, kerosene,
rat poison, busted coulters, buckets of bolts,
and coffee tins of whatever else had slipped
from hands, my father's farm-hard hands,
silent and desperate with the threat of rain.

CALF-MIX CUPS

Come calving time up in Wisconsin,
semi-trailers would pour south to our county
with loads of bawling, just-weaned calves.

You could hear them for miles through
foggy winter mornings, hear them for miles.
We'd rig up a barn with gates and feeding stalls,

then, twice each day, cycle their hunger through,
mixing formula from red-checkered sacks
with steaming water, rubbing their damp muzzles,

turning them into pets, then steaks or money.
In each bag of calf-mix was a plastic measure,
and the plywood cupboards in every church

in Fulton County were stacked high with them.
Come snack time at Bible school or revival,
the cups were born again away from the tongues

of baby Holsteins, and each became a child's
salvation: after hot preaching the children fled
to the dank concrete addition where cups

of many colors waited with sweet Kool-Aid,
liked by none, loved by us, after all that waiting
and wiggling through an hour of dumb grey wind.

Cups in hand, we cycled through to the parking lot
for skinned knee games of freedom, growing as hard,
if not as fast, as the calves our fathers raised to cattle.

DRIVING WITH MY FATHER

Held tight between the old man's thighs
on a frozen January field, I learned
to steer a tractor.

My small boots dangled from the seat, but
I was driving, by God,
sighting the wheel down the furrow

toward a bent hickory in the fencerow.
I may've been three, no more,
when I learned these words,

the quiet vibrations
of the diesel's wheel, the power of an engine
awake in this small grip.

Tonight my son will take the pen
the old man gave to me,
I'll wrap my fingers tightly around his,

and we'll pull what only three men know
across a cold white field,
toward whatever trees may mark the line.

THE GLEANERS

> *"Thou shalt not wholly reap the corners of thy field,*
> *neither shalt thou gather the gleanings of the harvest . . .*
> *thou shalt leave them for the poor and strangers."*
>
> —Leviticus 19:9–10

We dragged our burlap sacks through bronzing fields
of stalks, without a thought that what we did
was blessed by God, scavenging the rows

like thickening coveys of crows behind fall
plowing. For each fifty-pound bag weighed-out
on the farmer's scales, we thought we stole

a dollar, and we could do it, too—maybe a dollar
each—in cut-up fields with points and corners,
where the combines balked and couldn't make the turns,

leaving ears, full, on stalks half-standing. Still
the taste of dry corn leaves parts my thighs,
my lips, with the kiss of fall and money.

Especially when the earth soaks dark with winter
rains, I envy the children, the birds we were,
shuffling tiny boots through dusk and yellow mud.

It would be a fair trade for the work we turn
to now, each aging winter, seeking, digging,
kicking crushed stalks for a blessing.

CLEANING SEED

Harried, young, and hungry for land,
my father was a hard man to look in the eye.
Each glance sliced like a tungsten blade.
Even his kind words dropped like curses.

In time I believed I'd caused his silence
by my worthlessness, and it sat in my gut
like heavy biscuits. When I left home,
I took a keepsake that I would hold close

to my chest: one bitter winter night
I stood by him in the back shed, working
behind the alfalfa cleaner, waiting
while it wheezed and shook and coughed,

an old lion with palsy. The dust from its belly
blended with the early winter dusk
and mixed with the warmth of coffee
from a Ball jar, double sugar and real cream.

The muscles in my child arms were happy.
When the lion shook out a shovelful
I turned the top of each burlap sack under
like cuffs while my father scooped the seed,

each load scraping my knuckles,
oozing my worth with the signal of blood.
I have worn that night like a solitary gem
in a cast-off, pot metal setting, until today.

I was building a trellis, and my daughter
stayed nearby, holding the cross-pieces
in place and teaching me that my father, too,
must have loved the touch of my hands.

13

John Deere Green

A little boy's job was fetching cattle, a bigger boy's
painting gates. With my father you always knew

where you stood: work, and you were worth feeding.
So on the longest August days that burned white-hot

by noon, he'd lean a dozen gates and sideboards
against the tractor shed before he left for his fields,

and he'd tell me they would be painted before supper.
By noon my hands and arms were John Deere green,

but I was a man, useful and oily and hungry
and beginning to see visions in the quivering heat.

It was sometimes more than I could do, and the paint
would soon creep up my arms, stretching my skin

like a drumhead. Only straight gas and a horse brush
would loosen enough to let me eat or take a drink

of iced tea. By evening I was sure the work could not
be done, and the sun and gasoline would burn

me blind for my labor. But coming home from his own
day's load, he'd take an old brush and help me finish,

even as the green turned gold in the baking rays of evening.
And so my sweat dripped with his, and I was thankful,

cleaning brushes in the emerald stones of the barnyard.

BROGANS

They were perfect shoes for farm boys.
Thick enough to carry you over
thorny bottom ground, high enough
to guard your ankles from burrs,
short enough to lace fast, just ahead
of your father's anger, the grey
of his weather, the leather smooth enough
to take polish, to shine for church—
no one I ever knew had two pairs.

For good or ill, they marked you.
May as well have tattooed a pig
across the shine of your forehead.
Your teachers knew the first day,
without knowing your name,
just where you were from.
Even visiting preachers knew
if you were worth a dollar. Not.

We made it by with common soles,
and I think some of us may yet
muck our way to heaven. Most
boys left theirs in bus stop lockers,
bought something cheap and slick,
and left the farm behind. Others,
like me, drag ours through cities still.
It all depends on how your toes turn,
how you wear what you've been given.

WINTER PLOWING

Rabbitting down in the seat of a John Deere,
my smooth boy cheeks thawing in the engine heat,
the waves of heat-houser canvas filling my nostrils,
sweetening my coffee with diesel smoke—
the steady cycling roared above the radio brogue
of LBJ and the boys from my church dying.
Mornings I slept through school, then afternoons

and evenings and nights I plowed, driving, lifting,
turning the frozen crust, keeping one front wheel
in the new furrow, near sleeping, almost dreaming
the letters prayed aloud on Wednesday nights
of jungles and greens our February could not believe.

Come dusk my mother's truck would lurch across
the new-plowed ground with side-meat sandwiches
and root beer in a can, and together we listened
to the radio, deaf to the falling of the hawk behind me,
blind to the whirl of his gyre, his waiting, waiting
for whatever might run from stalks not yet turned under.

All Good Things

My father was out the door by dawn to pump diesel,
to load his truck with fertilizer and seed.
When the help ambled out by six,

he was long gone, heading into the first sun.
And if the soil was fine and harrigated even
and the rock-picker boys had done a good job

and the ground was not wet but holding moisture,
why, by God, how *could* you spend a better day?
Even as he scooped those tons of nitrogen

into rusty planter boxes, he remained convinced
that such a life of work was all the proof
he'd need of God—and the only proof he'd take.

His greatest doubt was sown and fertilized
by the notion of a *superior* being who'd offer
something as worthless and sacrilegious

as a sabbath. So Sundays, too, his daughter or wife
would carry his dinner to the field, then supper,
and he'd eat on the tractor seat. On the best days

he'd quit after planting a hundred acres, then sit
and brood on the outside step of the mudroom,
grinning at the hands who drank in silence and

collapsed at the pump. Unlacing his high boots,
he'd babble on about work and weather and theology,
half puzzled at our weariness. But we took pleasure,

too, in his generous conclusion: how all good things
must grow together, work and love, love and work,
one old man, two boys, and thirteen hundred acres.

The Way My Father Farmed

after weeks of Wendell Berry

The great Kentucky poet claims it was wrong
to farm the way my father learned to farm,
clearing out fencerows, shooting the ground full
of nitrogen, spraying for broadleaf weeds

and grass and insects and God knows what else,
all to pull two hundred bushels off an acre
of hillside, forsaking cows to the dairymen
and beef to the giant western feedlots.

Wendell's right. The way my father farmed
was hell on women and good horses, and one
of the women was the earth herself. She paid
for how he plowed her: cancer, dead creeks,

a bad heart. But was there some blessedness,
too, in all that persistent attention—
one small man dying slowly in Ohio,
doing his damnedest to feed a hungry world?

SUPPERTIME

Just after autumn dusk its roar would crouch
along the gravel road, and from the haymow
window we'd spot it: my father's combine,
its lights sliding like a city through new-moon dark.
So the fodder at last had grown too tough

and suppertime could come. He'd cut the engine
behind the barn, beside the diesel tanks,
then ease himself down steps on cold steel hips
and ask us if we'd fed the steers and hogs,
checked the gates. I can't imagine saying *no*.

Some days he'd toss a sack half full of rabbits
from the cab, and say, *I believe I'll let you boys
clean those and take'em in to Mom*, and we would,
me holding the stiffening feet, getting peed on,
my brother wielding the knife. This was our life.

When our hands were scrubbed and the rabbits clean,
we sat down at the table, to meat and biscuit,
and he would count and tell how many acres of corn
he'd shelled, and what he thought it might make
per acre, unless the bottoms were thin. I can see him

now, leaning on his left arm, eating with the right,
his talk fading into a picture I carry here. Right here.

THE GRIP

The last time I knelt to shake
my father's hand, it was already
quivering a little, and the calluses
he'd earned with wrenches and shovels

and years of sixteen-hour days,
holding on to land and respect,
some of his children, and the torn
pages of a tired faith, had turned

to paper. It was hot, too hot,
a piss-dripping midwestern
August morning, hell on dogs
and just fine for money and corn,

and outside you could hear
a thousand acres of green stalks
wagging their tassels for water and light.
But his grip was loose like a bad

boy's whose mother makes him shake
with the preacher on the front step,
or a bankrupt's first *howdy* back home,
and his gunmetal eyes were empty

and grey, the color of Bokes Creek,
frozen over. And it was that grip
more than his shortened frame,
his missing foot, his beard-dark cheeks,

that told me my own father had let go.

WHERE IS MY FATHER NOW?

My childhood holiness nightmares
would say, *Afire in the flames of hell.*
Or maybe on the outside chance
that he was one of the truly elect,
Dancing his new translucent body
down a golden street, plucking a harp.
The bookishness of college years
offers some other language, maybe
Awake in the light of Divine Presence,
drifting through an extra-dimensional
cosmos in a prelapsarian condition of bliss.

Some tribe somewhere must have better stories,
stories of green hills and fishing,
'coon to hunt, or better yet, a farm
where crops move through their cycle
and a glorious John Deere pulls
perpetually well-greased plows
through golden fields of stalks left
by two-hundred-bushel-per-acre corn,
and the air is as chilly as the sun is bright
and the only smoke is in his smokestack
and the only music is the engine's low whine.

THE END OF THE HOMEPLACE

On afternoons when fool's gold weighs
its worth on me, the old house rises
to stand as it stood the day I rented a car
in Dayton and drove until stone roads
narrowed into home. And there it was,
the west wind pouring through its eyes,
a clapboard death's-head, the glass
gone from the windows, not broken
but removed, and when I drove past
again the next day, the roofing smoked
in a tarry heap above the cellar hole.

Today I'd like to leave this blue screen
and drive further still, to the places
rented cars don't go, to a dooryard
singing with children and a barn alive
with the bawling of feeder calves,
their tongues lolling over the gates,
hogs squealing, wallowing fresh mud,
a few dozen chickens squawking about
the price of eggs—a calendar print
I'd tried to hang twenty years before,

when boys were angry and bound to go
but I vowed to the creek and sycamores
to stay right there and be true to home.
Sometimes I see the house like that,
the day I swore it to myself, before
I turned toward those broader roads
and drove until the concrete turned
so hard and wide and only went one way.

Part II

CARDS ON THE FARM

Mostly in winter the family gathered
for food and photographs and cards.

Once the Olympics of eating were done,
tables all cleared and new coffee brewed,

the closets gave up their euchre tables,
drawers trickled forth a half-dozen decks,

ashtrays appeared, and the real work began.
Boys sent home for evening chores returned

with *Hell's bells, are you stuck with me?*
and *Give the old woman a stick and a basket!*

The cards were cussed, the tables knocked,
and the crazier cousins would jump up

and circle their chairs to change their luck.
Jesus Criminy, who dealt this mess?

And why not? The fates who could deal you
a loner or fill your hand with nines and tens

were the same ones who'd send an inch
of pounding rain to ruin your new-cut hay

and miss your neighbor one farm down
whose corn was curling for lack of a drink.

It's like that: your truck breaks down Monday,
and hauling your hogs a day late costs you

a year's profit. Or the president, in a moral fit,
embargoes grain to China, and it costs you

a tractor, a farm, a way of life. Why not
smoke another Lucky, eat another piece of pie,

deal another hand? Why not enjoy a raucous
chance on something that doesn't really matter?

And why not try like the devil himself to win?

MERLE FREEMAN'S AUCTION

John Deere grain drill, Farmall Super H, complete dairy
set-up, household goods too numerous to mention.

With land prices rising, they all said,
"Raise the ante and bet on rain."
So he did, and he didn't save his face
cards, and he lost the trick, the hand,
the tournament. Today they sell the chips,
the table, the tractors, the milkers.

The hearts of his days were dealt away in fields
and barns, but today it's the household goods
that hurt him most to see knocked down—
white carnival vases, ruby hummingbirds,
the pressure cooker, the cribbage boards.
His landlessness will trump him later.

Neighbors wander through his halls,
as if they'd never laughed in these rooms
or sat for supper, or tipped these chairs
around the euchre table. They've come
to take their chances, to find a bargain.
No one reneges. And no one's bluffing.

Shoot me, says the man who didn't believe
in poker. *Shoot me, you bankers, lawyers,*
neighbors—you thin-blooded batch of kibitzers.

First Snow

The barn was sixty quiet paces through
the dark, beyond the mudroom lights that fell
across this first unlikely, early snow.
He looked ahead to what must be, then back
inside to what had been. He knew the woman
wasn't quite asleep, but he had waited as long
as he could wait, had taken all he could take.
Above, the tatted lace of new-moon stars
promised him something of a world to come.
He turned toward the stables, first his feet,
then his aching plastic hips and worthless heart.
He meant, he thought, to stop it all, right here,

the nauseating ache, the taste of coins,
sweaty pennies, and this, the old feeling
he'd had before, when his brother used to grab
the loose flesh on his arm and twist and twist
until he swore *uncle*. But now the arm
was his chest. And there were other aches as well—
a daughter good as dead, his sons who wouldn't speak,
and most of all the woman, waiting for him now
to check the horses. She'd hated him, he believed,
since first they lay together, south of Traverse Bay.
The wind off Michigan stung their bodies with sand.
No song, no lie, had ever since consoled her.

Inside the gate he felt for the can in the barrel
and shook a pint of oats for Tucson Jim,
the pacer that had been for him the candle

at the end of these dark months. He'd won
every race they'd staked him to—by God
he could've won the Jug. The pair stood dazed
in cold November. He stroked and scratched
Jim's flanks, glad now that all the flies would die
with this first taste of winter—how they drove
him mad in June. So this is it, he thought,
an old man and his first fine horse. For a moment
he could not remember what had carried him
to the barn, until he felt the halter rope knotted
in his hands, one end dangling over the beam.

THE SEASON OF HEAVEN

You've got to forgive a mortician
for doing his business. Those lips
were painted and ratcheted into a grin,
almost twitching, thin and pink and not

Merle Freeman's, whose dusty mouth knew
three expressions: one of them mean,
one of them mad, the other a grimace.
Above the coffin, an old card shark,

one he'd starched and ironed in better days,
grinned: *Merle sure looks natural, don't he?*
And another added, choking the lie,
Don't know as I ever saw him in a tie.

But you can't bury even a farmer in overalls.
His fingers looked like they needed grease.
The ruddy burn that colored his cheeks
beneath the shadow of his Ohio Grain cap

was already fading into grey. But that smile . . .
who would've thought his lips could do it?
Maybe the season of heaven is August,
and Merle is over his head in four-dollar corn.

In Praise of Cowards

No brave man could ever imagine
how much a coward can tolerate.
No hero could ever bear so much:
so many tiny bottles, tinctures of horror
to be shaken in bitter, stale water

and swallowed without flinching,
so many quick little razor slits
in his itchy scrotum. A coward learns
to tolerate any flagellation
from whatever strong arm flicks the whip.

The religion of daily drudgery,
the slowly broken spine of hope—
a brave man would run back to the mountain
and hide his heroic head in shadows,
but any coward learns to bear it.

So praise him, the boy who never knows
the quick, passing pain of a broken arm,
who never knows the beauty of the view
from the top of the tree. He learns to live
with loss, and, likely as not, to smile.

Miss Tuttle's Sixth Grade, Fulton Elementary

Miss Tuttle was the captain of her class.
Her fierce insinuations maintained her rank,
her contempt for sloppy cursive, mumbled words,
for fools, *small fools*, who fail to carry the three.

Farm boys didn't mind their knuckles rapped,
but it was hard to untangle the shame,
so at noon they'd head out to the football field
to trade their anger for some good clean pain.

By sixteen they were primed to leave school,
but with Goodyear and Whirlpool laying off
or closing down, there weren't many places
to go. And there were always recruiters around.

Must I assume that none, none *of you recall*
Cambodia is west, west *of Vietnam?*
Most of them know that now, Miss Tuttle,
though they may not come home to tell you.

Buzzards Wheeling

Their pale white lives were nothing like news.
On those over-tilled Midwestern plains
where factory farms had driven most
of the critters away, a deer in the ditch

or a stray coyote was high drama.
So when the boys saw buzzards wheeling
and their father hadn't put them to a job,
they'd hop on their bikes and pedal hard

toward ground zero. They had to know.
Roadkill was easy to find, though sometimes
little was left and they had to guess what—
squirrel or rabbit, 'possum or 'coon?

On other days the dead would rest
in a corn field, and they'd pitch their bikes
in the ditch and race down tunnels of green,
guided by the gyres of the scavengers

and eventually by their own noses.
Even when knowledge meant a mile
of kicking through bottomland brush,
too wet, too thorny, or too low to farm,

they had the need to know. So that's how
they found John N. Doe—the name
their father learned from the deputy
who showed up early the next day.

John N. Doe was the first black man
those two farm boys had ever seen,
and they never learned why he was dead
in their ash thicket above the water gap.

A Boy and His Dog

His cheeks flush red when he walks by the widows
wreath, by the basin in the dust where the old dog
lay through all nine years of August afternoons.

He rakes it sometimes, that circle of dirt between
the bushes and steps where nothing grows.
It's only dust on a farm that is dust, and he is dust

as he works it. But he reddens, not with heat,
but because he quit his chores too soon and left
the hayfork turned out, so that when the collie chased

by after a rat, he flipped the fork into his own belly
and dragged it through the barn, impaling himself
more deeply with each frenzied lunge. The image

remains, as does the run to the house for the gun,
fumbling, counting seventeen shells in the tube,
the wait for a clean shot that wouldn't come, it would

not come, twenty seconds, maybe, or ten, that passed
as slowly as the last point of a bad sermon, or the last
chorus of "Just as I Am Without One Plea," then

he emptied the rifle into the whining beast, its body,
though he knew that an old dog takes a lot of killing,
and, even then, where it would run at last and lie down.

He sickens with the memory, the negligence
first, but then, how he couldn't get a good shot.
And what his father thought and could not say.
And how glad he was to see that house burn down.

The War in Ohio

Our Vietnam was locked in a cabinet
of brown plastic, almost purple, a Zenith
the color of a bruise. Pull the switch,
and it would stretch open its eye
until all Southeast Asia was awake
in our front room, a rainforest so green,
a green so deep you could almost see it
in the grey tones of the swollen screen.

Lists of numbers settled at the bottom
as a man who hid behind a mustache
talked about our boys and their boys,
the essential statistics, the casualties,
the missing, the wounded, the dead.
In school I would learn that we beat
them right up until the day we lost.
Push the switch, and the eye would close,

quickly first, then increasingly slowly,
until all of Asia was nothing but a light,
a single spot at the center of the glass,
and my thoughts turned back to Ohio,
to the new Holstein calves, a truckload
we'd just hauled in from Wisconsin,
bucket calves that would be suckling
from racks of galvanized pails in our barn;

and to the Western Flyer bike I'd seen
during a *word from our sponsors*—a dream
that would never travel our stone road;
and then to the scent of our supper
boiling in the kitchen and the sharp tap
of a heavy spoon or ladle on the edge
of a stainless kettle, a banging that rang,
for all the world, like a gunshot.

THE MAN WHO SHOOTS STOP SIGNS

Standing alone on a dark road, maybe he believes
the new ones are virgins, too hard to resist.

Or maybe his girlfriend told him *Stop*, and he did,
but he didn't like it. Tonight he hates the word.

Or maybe he got lucky at a yard sale, bought a six-pack,
and drove around to celebrate his new used .22.

Or maybe it had to be the sign or his dad, and his dad
was never home. So he made do with the sign.

Or maybe, as ugly as Vietnam was, there are parts
of it he misses, or wishes that he could've missed.

Or maybe if your nights are bad enough, you don't
want to be told what you already know. Whatever.

Whoever walks these roads will know you were here,
that you found another way to sign your name.

WHAT HE NEEDED

That house had everything he needed. Sometimes
the smell of a Winston in the wind, or the closed-in
scent of hominy frying and chicken from a can
could carry him to the place where Grandpa Tom
must have sat on the back step and laced his shoes,
not to work, but because a neighbor needed a hand
with a down cow; or, that done, because the folks
on the Hanson place with both boys finally home
were having a kitchen dance and they wanted
a fiddler. Maybe he could get Tilly to second him,
if Frank didn't mind, and Ma could take the girls.

Even after Tom had died, the house had everything.
Where the last two—Charlie, with his bad hand,
and Pearl, barely married once—sat to wait for news
and death, suppertime and *As the World Turns,*
small and black and white, he could see the packs
of Teaberry gum on the pump organ, the walnut
gingerbread, even the dowel where Tom's fiddle hung.
And he could get close enough, when Charlie dozed,
to rummage the drawer for cigarettes and French harps
and a pulp magazine called *Country Song Roundup.*
It had interviews, and "all the words to all your favorites."

And on top of the cupboard—or was it beneath her bed—
was Pearl's autoharp, the one she ordered from Sears,
and the *Songs and Memories of Columbia Recording
Stars—Flatt and Scruggs and the Foggy Mountain Boys.*
So it didn't matter where he was lying today—
Ohio, Kansas, Canada, New Jersey, Vietnam—

he left there many times to take another glance
at this page or that, to sneak into a cupboard,
to sniff the stale and hazy air, to steal a cigarette,
to double-tongue a tune on Uncle's rusty harps,
to find these pictures that might still fit his words.

MILKING IN THE DARK

With the second glance down,
Hazel's hand gripped the child's
casket, her curly black head
dropped, and she shook. Then

her belly pitched a fit as though
she'd been kicked, kicked by a cow
or a mule or plow horse, just above
her waist. The left knee buckled,

then the right. Her red-faced
husband, dull in new black,
reached an arm behind her,
not gracefully. He too was bent

with milking and grief and
after all, it was the first touch
like that she'd ever needed.
How could he have been ready?

Their boy dead—it had come at last.
Hazel caught herself in a space
between two heaves of storm
and sank her nails into the wood.

That was the first time. Now
the chickens don't have feed
some days, and the gate hangs
by one hinge. The cow bawls.

Because she asks, each afternoon
her man drives her by that room
they use instead of church, even
here where people try to believe,

where for her that night remains
forever, the night they wept
in dark new clothes and shoes
that didn't fit, the night her knees

gave way, the night she felt an ocean's
rolling weight against her chest,
her gut, her womb. Home again,
she squats beside a doe-eyed Jersey

and leans her cheek against its flank.
She rubs the heavy bag until at last
the milk eases down, released
by the touch of her inarticulate hands.

FARM WIDOW

She stands in his sheep barn,
where the smells of wool and urine
have not and will never go away,
but will stay in the wood of the beams
and the cracked concrete of the floor
until her sons tear the barn down,
and ever after,
people driving by will say
"That was Elmer's sheep barn, there."

She, Elmer's old woman,
will be dead by then,
would be dead now if she had her way:
she has come to the barn to cry.
At noon she went to the cellar and found
a can of berries that he'd picked,
and she smiled, and could not eat them,
and she cried and retched,
then came into the sheep barn.

She knows well that people
who write songs and TV shows
and such foolishness about lovers dying
are liars, that it's not beautiful
like they make it out to be, not at all.
It hurts until you don't even know
if the fifty-three years you had
together, though they were pretty good,
pretty much, were worth—this.

Explanations for the Night

Her doctor, she says, claims he can't do a thing
for her other troubles until she starts to sleep.
Anybody who goes a day or two without it
is likely to forget things, lose things, maybe
even find things that aren't really there.
You take that prescription, he says, let yourself
get some rest, and your house will quit talking.
His pen ticks like a clock against his clipboard.

Her grandson has stayed two nights to listen.
A lot of things, he says, can make a house talk.
The furnace coughs before the blower starts
and the ducts crackle when they cool down.
Drafts whisper through the vents if there's wind,
and your darn freezer is a regular church social.
Sometimes, he says, you even leave your TV on.
Maybe, she tells him. Maybe not. But a widow,

at least an old one, doesn't have much to do
at night but worry, and she has lots of things
to wonder about. Sometimes fear's better than
other things it might be—memories have a way
of ganging up on you. And she does not say
that if it's Elmer, coming back or never left,
she mostly wants to hear him, to hear what
he has to say for himself. To tell her why.

THE BLUE PLATE

Late evening she leans on the countertop.
Grounded in her kitchen, she can still feel
what goes where, put her few things away.

Not enough exercise and too much work—
never a morning free to keep a proper garden—
then diabetes, blood pressure, all that weight.

Tonight her fingers won't bend. They flap about
the cup handles like stray, sad tongues.
She drops a plate. It breaks. Bending over

to pick it up is slower than lowering a bridge.
Once that's done she'll go to bed, where she can lie
awake and listen to the empty sounds a house makes.

Her hopes of growing old and dying at home flee
with the evenings. She'll soon be a number to check
on some nurse's chart, a body to be lifted and fed,

heaved onto a bedpan, bathed before the shift
changes or her family visits. Age, she believes,
is like a puzzle no one can do, or some movie

you didn't understand then: Jake Barnes goes off
to France and meets that Brett woman again,
the one who knows that love can't really happen

no matter how much she wants it. Now she knows
no woman can keep what she needs the most:
this farm, her own kitchen, even that damned blue plate.

Part III

The Old Ways

My granny could conjure off a wart
with a soup bean. Most other ailments
could be borne or healed with gravy.

She knew lots of old ways, I'm sure,
but she could only trust me
with so much. I'd found too much religion,

too young. She didn't go to church often,
but when she did, she sat by me and sang.
Now *she* was a *hymn singer*, so ice-pick loud

it'd winch up the corners of your mouth—
but I was too amazed to grin,
so full of wonder at what God had wrought

and glad to be rid of the warts on my fingers.

Songs We Live By

When Tilly got old, she wrote down words
to songs she'd sung forever, the ballads, yes,
she'd learned as a girl, but others, too,

from Jimmy Rodgers and the Carter Family,
songs she'd carried like her mother's dishes
from county to county and house to house.

Her daughter, the girl who did office work,
typed them up neatly in little books.
I didn't understand her quirky turn then,

but these days it makes sense, as I sit here
with her old banjo and a little less to sing,
my own friends fading away like dreams

that disappear with coffee. It's not quite
like dying, but you know what's coming.
And you want to slow it all down,

to rub your fingers over etched patterns,
chipped gilt edges, the cool touch of milk-
glass smoothness, translucence that recalls

an old woman's face, a patched dress,
a mothering hand warm against the back
of your neck, a cheek you'd gladly kiss again.

Patch's Wife

Her eyes turned dark that first winter
after Abel was born, though Patch
could not see how, with the new light

of their son brightening each room,
she could say the world was a mine
and her life just coal, *dirty old coal.*

But their house sat back from the road
at the edge of a wood, and the trees
waved dismal shadows at her miseries.

The next winter, with the boy weaned
and her already big with Evaline,
was only worse. Patch wrung his hands,

afraid of what he might find in the cellar
when he came in after milking each night,
or when he rode home late from fiddling

or calling figures for a dance in town.
But if he suffered from his own dread,
he suffered more for her, and he swore

he'd move the earth to make it right.
Then, since the earth just wouldn't move,
he thought, *By God, I'll move the house.*

He swapped out his promise of work
with neighbors and borrowed their teams.
They cut beams and spaced out rollers,

and in a week the old house stood
on new block pillars by the main road.
After that he said it creaked a bit,

but stood straight enough for living in.
At least a few cars passed there, a few
wagons. And when she spelled herself

on the porch, quilting or shelling peas
or nursing their third, and when the river
behind her eyes would rush and roar

and her legs would prickle and go numb
and make her want to die, she had
one steady rope to hold, forever:

a memory of mules hitched in gangs
snorting and straining at their collars,
of the grind the crossties made on logs

with the creaking, screeching cables,
of a dozen strong men skidding beams
or sprawling wasted by the pump,

and, mostly this: the bright-eyed love
of a one-eyed fiddler who swore
he'd move the world for her, and he did.

His Last House

At last Frank found a house that faced the creek,
paid cash, and moved in. It was too square,
but she would've liked the way the porch looked

toward the road, and the stove sat on a pad
of field stone. It would do. He bought a chair
that fit him well, and figured he'd never need

to move again unless he had a mind to.
On sunny winter mornings, he drove back
to the creek to cut a little brush, culled out

whatever was stove-wood size, and lit the rest.
Some days he brought sausages, as he did
before he was married. Back then, he'd roast frogs

or rabbits, even crawdad tails, if that
was all there was to be had. A long time ago.
At home he stirred the stove and fried three eggs

and thought of how Tilly used to sing herself
around the kitchen while she cooked. Today
he'd like to taste her bread again. His neighbor

sometimes stopped over with donuts after work,
and he wished he could've visited with him some,
but never could, all his life, think of what to say.

She had always talked, and he had kept
the fire going. There were still some days
when both could do their parts as well as ever.

The Woman with the Wooden Arm

As a bride she'd chosen the worst of all times
to wedge between a cow and the wall of a barn.
Her shoulder was crushed, her arm badly set,
and the child she was bearing, her only and last,
was lost. The stiff branch dangled the rest of her life.

So she would work. With her good strong left
and the oak-stiff right that throbbed her memories,
she would swing an axe, and, come harvest time,
cook for an army of thrashers, without complaint,
almost, but never quite, beyond their notice.

Her husband wanted sons and she could not.
One day he was gone—Oklahoma was the rumor—
and she was left with his mortgage and her will
to live. She sold off what she couldn't handle
and she never missed a due date on the note.

Old, you could see her yet, swinging a slop bucket
over the hillside, crawling down a berry row
with a basket slung across her breast, husking corn
with the stalk tucked under her crooked wing.
Morning and evening, she made her rounds

of the beasts she loved, pumping water, mucking stalls,
splitting bales for bedding, pouring oats and ear corn,
and shuffling her way to the old milking stanchions.

Brother Everest Cleans His .22s

When he hunted, he kept the muzzle down
and turned away from his companion,
away even from his beagles that sang the trail.
In the seconds before he fired, he scanned
the horizon and knew the arc of every pellet's flight.

When he popped targets with his boys in open range,
he always found a steep bank, then hauled out
a quarter sheet of half-inch plywood and leaned it
against a tree. When the shooting was done,
and his sons were bathed and sleeping, his wife in bed,

waiting, he'd take the guns to the milk shed alone
and light a lantern. There he'd check each chamber
two or twenty times for unspent shells,
and even then, he kept the muzzles pointed toward
the floor or a solid wall, naturally, easily, in a way

unknown to men who have never shot their fathers.

Collector Glass

Frank's big fingers were as rough as the files
he handled every day, and his tongue—
the one he used at work—was rougher yet.

He worked as a carpenter, and he worked
on a section gang for the Lackawanna,
and, when he got old, he plated toilet parts

with chrome for Elgers. Two bucks an hour.
At home he'd go a week without speaking
and when he bothered to talk, his voice was

a wire brush on a stubborn bit of rust.
But if you bothered to ask, and some did,
he could whisper you a little more than

you really wanted to know about cobalt
or ruby, carnival or amethyst, his calluses
detailing and lips praising a hundred pieces

of depression he kept in a cupboard he built
by the window. Some mornings as he leaned
over coffee, grits, and sausage, dreading the day,

the sun caught them just right, and he would
waken to the light of all those gentle rainbows.

What Tilly Knew

Tilly knew what she knew.
She could bake good light bread—
being born with the hands for it.

With vinegar and newspaper,
she could clean windows like
a white slave, which she'd been.

She could conjure a wart off
your finger with a soup bean,
if you were truly willing.

Outside, she could care for stock
and keep a Yankee garden, cut trees
and make wood, though she often

praised God for coal oil stoves.
And because her man had the habit
of selling whatever wasn't tied down,

she'd offer you dime-store mints
in a crystal dish. "Lord, Billy,"
she said, "you may as well use it."

Hanover Lindy and the Miracle

O Death, where is thy sting?
O Grave, where is thy victory?

Most pacing horses never make the grave.
They show some promise for two or three years,
stir stories in the tack room coffee while they can,
travel some, win a little bit with any luck,

then fall away through lower stakes and pass
through claiming races and county fairs. Finally
it's the food chain, chopped for American dogs
or broiled as steaks for the Quebecois.

And that's just how Hanover Lindy went.
Small to start with, and pale white feet,
she'd never've been much. Her lungs gave out,
and she started bleeding through her lasix.

But Rufus Steck said, poised on a tack box,
She does, I believe, know how to put her ears back.
So her owner went to Canada and bought
a miracle. Two days after, Half-Track Mosher,

who mucked the stalls, swore, *Dat horse run
a hole in da wind, she 'bout outrun da buggy.*
The next time Rufus took her out himself,
and hostile watches clicked in every stable window

like you'd stomped a bag of pretzels. It worked.
But only twice. The bleeding started again.
She could lead at the half, but never win.

So that was that. But there's plenty of folks
around the grounds, like Rufus and Half-Track,
who, all their lives, were two-six pacers
in a two-minute world. And they think about her yet,
how her feet always hurt, but how she put her ears back.

WALTER MACK, RELOADING

In from the fields, he would sit on the steps
of the mudroom, unlace his high boots
with fingers raw from the cold, then limp
to the sink and wash the land from his face
and arms and hair. After coffee and pie,
he'd drift back to a table in the shed where
he kept spent 12-gauge shells, tins of powder,
boxes of wads, and canvas bags of shot.

With the help of the man on the radio,
he dreamed about winter and reloaded shells.
Though he shot registered trap and skeet
with a handicap, and sometimes made up
special loads for windy days or tough targets,
he reloaded mostly for its own sake,
for the rhythm, steady and quiet and sure,
of the machine's long arm pressing down—

and for the solitude such habits bring.
I thought it strange, then, and would now,
were it not for this turning I feel,
when a day full of words has fired holes
in my faith, to linger in a warm dark barn,
fingering some tool. When Walt died
he left three sons who mourned their loss
with sad and busy hands, two debt-free sections,
and twenty thousand rounds stacked in pine crates.

UNCLE WALT'S SHOULDERS

Bull-necked Uncle Walt had shoulders packed
hard as gunny sacks tromped down full,
strength he savored because, he claimed,
as long as he could do two hundred push-ups,

he could eat whatever he damn well pleased,
whether Aunt Winny, who was the school nurse,
part-time, in the north end of Fulton County,
said it was healthy or not. She said *not*.

So he was the only man I ever saw cook,
and every morning, too: a tube of biscuits
and gravy rivers without end. Such arms
were blessings on a farm. He could catch you up

quick if you got behind stacking back hay,
then hop down from the mow and work the wagon.
If calves balked at the loading shoot, he'd heave
them into the truck. And when the ground froze

in January, he was God's own lumberjack.
He could squat and cut with a long-blade saw
all morning without a break. The only help
he needed was a kid to drag brush away

and load the truck. So I was there beside him
the day he cut a honey locust off fence-high—
it had grown around the old wire—and the butt
slipped the stump and jumped back into his chest.

The scream of steaming air quitting his lungs
was loud, as loud as the crack of the tree's hinge
against his ribs. I eased my rolled coat beneath his head,
and blood seeped from his lips and ears and gathered

in his dimples like roses, his face as white
as ice, those shoulders soft and strangely still.

The Duty of Crows

"When Death comes," Hazel said, "it's best just to leave
the room and let it come." And she knew it would.
She'd seen the way wax dripped

from the Christmas candles, crooked and green,
and the way grey clouds hung above the barn
that morning, the shape and shade of marble.

Then the old fool let his truck get stuck axle deep
in the wood lot, though she'd told him the ground
hadn't froze enough to go back and cut,

but he'd said, as he always did, that he reckoned
he'd get out and do a job of work—
though things needed to be done inside, and he knew it.

Last fall he saw a horned owl perched on a shock
in the middle of the day, and he told her so,
not to worry her. Last summer, too, putting up hay

one evening, he swore he'd seen blue candles moving slow
above the pasture on Fulton Creek. And the crows—
they'd seen crows on the garden fence and rooftree.

It's the duty of crows to let you know, and they had.
"So when Death comes, it's best to leave the room and let it."
And then we knew what he had known for years,

that it wasn't our affair, that death is work you do alone,
though we didn't know how alone you needed to be.
While we waited in the kitchen, she showed us that.

Part IV

The Lovely Miss McKendry, School Librarian

She had the look of cash about her, so how
she landed in our school, it's hard to say.
Her lovely face, her body, were as out of place
among us as we felt about ourselves—
the outcaste handful who, though born to farm,
were fated not to take to hogs or corn,
or tear an engine down behind the barn,
or make sense of commodities markets.

Even then I knew I'd soon be leaving home,
but hardly knew a likely place to go.
So she gave me a key to her office,
a place to hide when classes moved too slow,
and I read everything that I could lay
hands on, most of it twice. One golden day
she cracked open the door, smiled and said
in a voice as sweet as rain falling on money,

"What else would you like to read? Anything?"
Those words still make an old prof's heart sing.
She'd found some shekels in a dead account,
and she told me I could pick a book out.
Just let her know, she said, she'd order it,
though it might be helpful not to mention it.
That was the best proposition of my life,
offered by the kindest face in my memory.

Maybe it was the romance of the blacklist
or because he sang a world I knew I'd missed,
but I chose Pete Seeger's radical red book,
The Incompleat Folksinger, a volume packed
with sufficient political entendre
to lead any young Republican astray.
Astray, just where I'd always hoped to go.
And the lovely Miss McKendry seemed to know.

Scholarship Boy

Even after all that education, the church folks
would say, then click tongues and shake heads
and feel honest pity as they watched his rusted-out

Datsun hobble down his daddy's lane, raising dust,
and limp on over to Turkey Foot Quick Mart,
where he'd buy gas and smokes, a six-pack

of Rolling Rock, two dozen meal worms
and three of those cellophane burritos
you heat up in the microwave by the coffee maker.

Then he'd drive up toward the holiness church
and park in their lot, if it wasn't Sunday
or Wednesday, and hike a hundred yards

to the old bridge. It was always cool under there,
and tiny stalactites dripped an ancient rhythm.
After dark he'd prod a small fire or blow the harp,

but mostly he just dangled worms for bluegill,
or, if they wouldn't hit, put on a nightcrawler
and let it settle on the bottom, watching until the line

would stand taut like the veins on his forehead,
then haul in a catfish or a fat old turtle, without
a hint of postmodern skepticism, or the more recent

views and revaluations of American naturalism,
or the imperative to form a less tyrannical canon—
all of which he understood and none of which

seemed to matter as much as the fire, the bridge,
the cut of the line in his palm. The neighbors didn't
know what to think, but figured it was a shame,

because they recalled him being saved, and wondered
what could have gone wrong up there in Columbus.

THE FARMER AND THE SILENT *S*

Back at the farm, how he talked didn't matter.
He could think all day on the tractor, stop
only for meals. Then he went to a university
where, right there in Philosophy 101,
he mispronounced two names in one sentence.
Camus and *Descartes*. Who the hell would've figured?

Someone laughed. Half the class, really, but especially
a woman with reddish hair and clearly no bra,
who had pronounced many names before,
even if she never did all the reading
and cheated on her tests. Her laughter was cold,
like a ball bat cracking ice in moonlight.

So he went to the library to appraise the situation.
He calculated his pages per hour by pages per book.
The numbers made his forehead hot
and the rest of him all clammy and cold,
like a carcass just skinned out, tossed in a bucket.
The next day he tried his advisor.

Dr. Culvert wore a plaid coat with striped pants,
the same coat each day, different striped pants.
He gave the farmer boy a tract, "Great Books of Our Culture,"
a ten-minute lesson on French pronunciation,
and then, because he was kind, a warning:
"You're only young once, and ignorance is forever."

That night he drank his first three beers, the next night
his second, etc. Mornings, alone, he would skip class
and go to Doobee's Used Records and Indian Imports,
just to thumble through the titles. In the heavy, sweet
scent of the old hippies, he sought the herbal cure.
He liked the way the album covers felt beneath his hand,

how everyone in the shop slumped, grey and baggy,
how loudly the music shouted from one stack to the next.
Each title, each psychedelic picture, offered many readings.
The records were clean and shone like the coulters of a plow,
and if some were deadly dull, some were just what he needed,
the fading grooves of art no one need ever memorize.

THE LANGUAGE YOU WERE BORN TO

You can fight it long enough, maybe,
to move *halfway* around the world,
to get *halfway* across the sea before
the motor sputters and spits, chokes,
and gives up one last stenchy cloud,
each gauge pegging left and in the red.

Maybe you're holding forth over
a napkin of wafers and Brie de Meaux,
sipping a half glass of something too dry
for your taste, but tolerable now since
your Phi Beta Kolleagues are nodding
toward whatever it is you're spewing

about the heretofore unobserved influence
of certain continental philosophers
on the uniquely American trajectories
of transcendentalism, some allusion
to Kant in William Ellery Channing's
lost journals. Then you sputter and slip:

I reckon y'all may be just a tad familiar
with that one little piece of Schopenhauer. . . .
Ah, that's when your sorry engine dies
and you're drifting in a blushing sea
of all you never were, mute in foreign waters,
wishing to God you'd stuck with the banjo.

Yes, All of It

My classes begin two minutes late.
Our little world has no central clock system,
and I've stopped fighting it.

So be here at 8:32, Tuesdays and Thursdays,
9:02 Mondays, Wednesdays, and Fridays.
That's close enough. Two minutes grace,

that's how I love you. Because I'm twice,
nearly thrice, your age, I've dreaded
and survived more future than you can

accurately imagine. This morning.
It wasn't worth the worry. But—
the present isn't all that great,

as those who've taken my surveys
can tell you. There's no legal escape.
So do come by 8:32 or 9:02,

and we'll push these clouded moments
into the past, where we can analyze them,
cherish them at a distance, even try

to understand why they concern us.
And regardless of when you come in,
how closely you pay attention,

and when you choose to leave,
it'll all be on the test. All of it.

THE PROFESSOR WHO LOVED BANJOS

A gentleman is someone who knows
how to play the banjo but doesn't.

—Mark Twain

Eventually the library lost its charm.
While colleagues sought the rarest variant,
he improvised, or wrote nothing.
Some days he even forgot his notes.

Then he'd simply bend the *B* string blue,
flat the thirds, open a fifth, and keep rolling
while his world-wise, senior majors grinned
their "But I'm immortal, thank you" grins.

And though each fall the freshfolks filed in
and crossed their fawnish legs, and nodded
in nubile confusion at the cut-time
syncopation of his morning lectures,

he never missed a chord or spent his tenure
on a bed. Each smile he saw was pearl inlay,
each pile of well-teased hair a golden flange,
and down below, maple necks and bird's-eye rims.

His pickup never crossed a bridge that wasn't
stretched with strings. His lawn was yellowed
with neglect, his back porch stacked with ancient
texts, and his garden? A tablature of crows.

HAVING MASTERED TIME TRAVEL, MARK TWAIN VISITS THE WALMART SUPERCENTER

No, he's not bewildered in the least.
He takes it all in at once, every snag,
every ripple, each flittering of light,
and sees in a single squint the genius
of scale, the lucrative convenience
of a single roof, how it would drown
every mom and every pop, the way
it would wash every little river town
downstream: it's sad, but the profits
appeal to him. He even likes the way
his shock of grey looks almost blue
in the buzzing lamps. And he likes
the carts piled high with stuff—shelves,
stacks, pallets, big damn lusty stern-
wheeled packet boats of products,
the aisles of anonymous plastic waste,
a mix of the necessary and profligate
proffered with equal absence of shame.
Mark is a moralist, but not one to let
his scruples slow the big wheels down.
He knows sometimes a big steamer
will overrun a raft just to see the splinters.
Plus, he always liked circuses, and this one
comes with miles of bread, cheap if not free.
He damns it all and spits in the corner.
He'll write about it. If the book sells
he'll buy shares: stock ticker *WMT.*

WHITTIER AT MIDNIGHT

Tonight let's think of Greenleaf in Amesbury, alone
and famous, already an icon, as beloved
for his virtue as his verse. But without a lover.

He must have taken up the stick and walked
the streets at night, he must have listened hard,
in the roar of mills, for God to speak again

as He had in the white heat of seedtime, when
He blessed the poet with cadence and a cause
that was true: his woe was the woe of the republic,

his song, the slave's song, the raven's call of war.
Would he never hear that sound again?
To the thud-tap of well-made boots on bricks,

what phrases traveled through his rhyming mind?
Which clichéd iambics stole his thoughts away?
Or did his sorrows never grow beyond that ache—

the loss, the years and words he spent on just
ideas, deprived of the touch of a thigh, of a kiss,
too deeply wrapped in the arms of Truth to wed—
or even much love—anything less than a country?

A Quiet Place to Pray

Simeon Stylites left his shepherd's manse behind,
but even the hut he built seemed just too lush.
With nowhere left to go *away*, he went *up*.
Still they came, the lovelorn, sick, and poor,
the curious and the kings. Thirty-seven years
on that pillar, and the pilgrims kept on coming.

Good Saint Henry built a cabin, quaint little place
facing the water, tidy pine desk, and the best—
a sunny step for meditations. Maybe a little close
to town for his taste, but it gave him space to write
about his sweet dead brother John, and of course
the other book. Disciples came, still come.

The blessed bhikku Kerouac bought himself a pack
and thought he'd hitchhike his way to the holy.
He found he had to keep moving his brakeman's boots.
Fast cars and freights. I hope he found the silence
he was looking for before he found the bottom
of the last bottle. The hipsters trace his exodus.

Our local Brother Martin, Trappist raconteur,
follows his ascetic way on Oregon's fairest farm,
prays hard among the gardens and wine vats,
sleeps behind the stone wall, comes out each day
to guide the spiritual way of professional wives:
the celibate guru of the lovely and young.

The hermit's burden? It's a trick to be alone.
Once people figure out you've pulled it off,
they can't seem to stay away. What's to say?
Isolation is one hot topic for conversation—
but it's more than nearly anyone can understand.
Most people want to learn about it secondhand. 73

ADVICE FOR A DIPSHIT COLLEAGUE WHO SHOULD KNOW

better. If you've set your heart on being a hound,

sleep beneath a porch, wander out when you hear
boots on the steps, then wander back under. Or

wake every house on the block by howling loudly
at some dung beetle every day for a week. Or

grab a shoe left on the step by your wife's yoga pal.
Run off with it. Chew it. Hide it. Bury it. Or

dig holes, a series of holes, a colony of holes,
a minefield of holes, an elocution of holes. Or

wait for a big fat moon, stray out to the sticks,
and chase possum all night. Or run 'coon. Or

whatever. The worst way is what you're doing now,
working your muzzle through a gaggle of bitches

as if your pretty bright wife didn't have a sense of
smell or a finger on either hand to phone a lawyer.

You'd be better off chasing semis. You'd be better
off catching one. Dive for the back side of a front wheel.

VANCOUVER WOMAN BEATS HER HUSBAND TO DEATH WITH A HAMMER

After *The Oregonian*, May 31, 2012

So how many times do you have to say,
"Don't leave those greasy dirty tools
on the dining room table, Sweetheart"?
Well, I guess somebody knows now.
At least he knew for half a minute.

Maybe he made the related mistake
of leaving his greasy tool on the bed.
Maybe he had it coming. Or maybe
he had it coming on some other bed.

It's a sad comment on these weird
and decadent days we die in.
What's become of the old-lace grace,
the gentility, of arsenic with tea?
Granted, critics call it sentimental.

You could take a more direct approach.
There's something akin to tenderness
in a .38 placed against a greying temple
dreaming sweetly of sugar plums.

Either way, the corpse could be a problem.
But since he always loved the garden so,
well, maybe he can stay there—it's poetry.
Think about him when you pull a turnip.
Whisper a little prayer. Say grace.

Or this: How about a broken brake line?
You can use his own damn coping saw
if, with that mess he leaves in the garage,
you can find it. Portland has plenty of hills.

Toss in some drama, a little pizzazz:
Call up the cop shop around midnight.
I'm so worried, he didn't come home,
he's never, never late. . . . Please, please. . . .
If theatre was never quite your shtick,

just hire a pro. There's simplicity
as well as commercial expediency
in a hired gun with a Heckler & Koch.
It's pricey, but you're buying a memory.

If that doesn't trip your trigger, maybe
you're destined to stick with tradition:
pure, icy contempt, dripping slowly,
silently, consistently for a long, long time.
But there's a certain mercy in a hammer.

Why We Keep Teaching

If you plod along the tenure track long enough,
a few of the lost come wandering back, just
as sure as Aunt Lydia's "Happy Birthday"
dollar or the ukulele you keep giving away
to every neighbor's toddler, or the yellow photos
of your hefty self you asked your wife to burn.

It's hateful August, and you're pining in a meadow
between mountains of paper spread over your desk,
pondering how best to fail at teaching comp
again, when your Macintosh wakes and beeps,
and *there it is*, that flicker of human contact—
a blinking, smiling message from your past,

this time a lawyer. Maybe your floundering stocks
have finally risen. Or your bonds have matured,
if not your poems. Maybe that sad old neighbor
whose car you used to jump-start has passed away
and left you three crates of *National Geographic*
and a million bucks. No, it's a former student.

"Thanks for everything," she writes. *And you're happy.*
That's how it is when they flicker back into your life,
sometimes to beg a reference, sometimes to tell you
they saw your name somewhere on the something.
Sometimes they even drop by campus to buy you lunch,
to feed you with the wonder of what they've become.

Making Bread, Making Do

The bread that God gives comes down
from heaven and brings life to the world.

—John 6:33

Last night I made white cornbread,
the iron-skillet, smoke-the-oil kind.
It's denser than yellow, maybe sweeter.
The grind feels finer to me.

If I want the bread to rise lighter,
I cut it with wheat flour, two to one.
More often, I mix yellow with rye,
and a quarter cup of sugar doesn't hurt.

Of course I make all sorts of biscuits.
I'll use white flour if there's company,
half whole wheat if they're just for food.
If I make them short enough, folks adjust.

And muffins? Sweet bran is my favorite,
but with soup I'll blend sorghum and corn,
then stir in a cup of sharp cheese—
that makes a hearty bread with protein.

You can see that mostly I do quick breads.
When I'm working, I don't take time
to fool with yeast, to let it rise up,
punch it down, rise again. I should.

I know it's prominent in Bible breads—
an infinitely metaphysical metaphor.
But leaven's not my concern just now.
When I worry the breads in the Bible,

John 6 is the one that troubles me,
the one that *brings life to the world,*
who claims to be the real bread—
those are his own words: *the real bread.*

What I'm cutting now seems real enough.
But somehow we all know there's more,
the way you sense you left the oven on—
and you *did.* In the meantime, I'll make do.

Mourning Ritual

Even on the fairest of mornings, like this,
some mildly neurotic grey man will fry
his eggs, grind coffee, butter his sensible toast,
and know the tenth of June won't come again.
He's leaving a world he's just begun to love.

He suspects a few acquaintances will gather,
that the closer of the lot, or more restive,
will share their anecdotes, feel something like hurt,
then leave to slog through everyday duties,
meetings and memos. A quick stop at Walmart.

If he's been moderately lucky, he can hope
his children fly home from somewhere to share
a modicum of memories, reasonable sorrow.
Their grief will be real, but they will bear it.
They'll leave with some cash and the better guitars.

And because all this is so stubbornly true,
I, too, am determined to love the way each dawn
fondles my sheets and to delight in the scratch
of the pencil's tip across the yellow page.
Bodies break. This I do in remembrance of me.

ON GOD'S TOOTH

What was it worth—that stony preaching of hell?
It drove you to prayer, no doubt about that.
It bred a schoolboy belief you never lost
even when faith had failed you, or changed

into something more akin to despair.
You dreamed the lips of fire, and you stood there
as your people were swallowed into waves,
those blood-red tongues, the sulfur breath of the tide.

You can't even say that it made you bitter
then. But you never met a friend who was not,
you were sure, near the gullet of eternal
pain, and you accepted as given their loss.

That done, you were swallowed with them, or worse.
Is that why you sit here now, on God's tooth,
scratching prescriptions on pale yellow sheets,
with only a mirror for company?

Waiting for the Specialist, I Dream of Fulton Creek

A miracle myriad of butterflies swarmed
in the mud at the crossing, where the fall
of spring floods left fetid pools and banks
exposed, a haven for insects and children,
a garden that never fell, made new that day.

With each small step or slap of a willow switch,
they consented to rise again. Like small gods
we called for whirlwinds, storms that rose and fell,
swirled and rose again, bright, like flurries of snow
in the headlights on a dark country road.

As many times as we urged them they rose,
changeless, blessing our persistent wills.
Lately I've been studying how life ends,
and now I dream of crossing to that place,
down a promised tunnel hollowed through years,

and the flash of those wings eases my way
forward, toward the tunnel's other end,
the final light that, so the mystics claim,
awaits the slap of each delighted stick,
the splash of each step, another age and garden.

Still Life with Banjo

One night with a little bit of bourbon
and the house empty, his wife gone away
to the coast (he'd never understood the coast),

he pulled his banjo from beneath the bed
and began to pick his catalog of tunes:
how he missed her but was glad she was gone,

his good job and why he had taken it,
his kind but sophisticated children
with straight teeth and well-worn passports;

then one about graduate school, eight years
of assuming a way of looking at books
that didn't suit how he felt about them

and, as he knows now from watching himself,
could never have fit a kid who showed up
on the land grant campus at seventeen,

with spackles of crick mud on his boots,
a Goodwill coat, and two new pairs of jeans,
never having made the ghost of a choice

but recalling a high school teacher's claim
that you need to leave to become somebody,
especially if you have a kind of *gift with texts*—

a promise he'd shown as the boy who didn't
take to tractor work. But his only memory
of feeling whole was when his grandmother,

sitting on the porch of a white frame house
near Magnetic Springs, admiring a fresh line
of blue shirts she'd just scrubbed on a board,

resting half a minute, had picked out a tune
then handed him the banjo and said, *Honey,*
I've an idee you're going to need this,

then took his pale hands in her red ones, said,
Here, put your fingers here. You go ahead.
And so he took it, and he went ahead.

Coda

At Rest in My Father's House

Before the window in a soft brown room
above the sunporch, my boy mind slept.
The house faced east toward Fulton Creek,
and each day faded easily to black,
alive with the winy dark of summer.

That was easy sleep, at rest in my father's house,
so gentle an embrace, so loose,
I mistook his easy grace for disconcern,
his hold so still, as sure as his feet
upon the earth, a love as ignorant as gravity.

That was my last real rest, in the dark
comfort of his silent, calloused love
that would not bear a fool, where night
was drawn away from my thrice-patched comforter,
and dawn rose bright and pale as an open palm.

ACKNOWLEDGMENTS

I thank the editors of the following publications in which some of these poems—often in slightly different form—first appeared:

ABZ: A Poetry Magazine: "Buzzards Wheeling," "A Boy and His Dog"

Appalachian Journal: "Still Life with Banjo," "Language You Were Born To"

Atlanta Review: "Having Mastered Time Travel, Mark Twain Visits the Walmart Supercenter," "The Lovely Miss McKendry, School Librarian"

Blue Collar Review: "The Barns"

Bryant Literary Review: "In Praise of Cowards," "The Man Who Shoots Stop Signs"

Cape Rock: "Merle Freeman's Auction," "The Season of Heaven," "Collector Glass"

Chaffin Journal: "Linea Nigra," "Advice for a Dipshit Colleague Who Should Know"

Chattahoochie Review: "Driving with My Father"

Clackamas Literary Review: "Vancouver Woman Beats Her Husband to Death with a Hammer"

Coal City Review: "Brogans"

Cold Mountain Review: "The Way My Father Farmed," "Songs We Live By"

Concho River Review: "Walter Mack, Reloading"

Connecticut River Review: "The War in Ohio," "Where is My Father Now?"

Cumberland Poetry Review: "Hanover Lindy and the Miracle"

The Distillery: "His Last House"

Evansville Review: "Milking in the Dark," "The Blue Plate," "Uncle Walt's Shoulders"

Flint Hills Review: "Making Bread, Making Do," "The Woman with the Wooden Arm"

Friends Journal: "Whittier at Midnight"
The Heartlands Today: "Suppertime"
The Journal: "The Duty of Crows," "Yes, All of It"
Literature and Belief: "Mourning Ritual"
Midwest Quarterly: "Cards on the Farm"
Natural Bridge: "What Tilly Knew"
Passages North: "The Grip"
Pennsylvania English: "Why We Keep Teaching"
POEM: "Waiting for the Specialist, I Dream of Fulton Creek,"
    "First Snow," "The End of the Homeplace"
Poetry Northwest: "A Quiet Place to Pray"
Roanoke Review: "The Old Ways"
Shawnee Silhouette: "Farm Widow"
Sou'wester: "The Gleaners," "Winter Plowing"
South Dakota Review: "Calf-Mix Cups," "All Good Things"
Southern Humanities Review: "Cleaning Seed"
Spoon River Poetry Review: "What He Needed"
Sun Dog: The Southeast Review: "The Professor Who Loved
    Banjos"
Weber: The Contemporary West: "At Rest in My Father's House"
West Branch: "Brother Everest Cleans His .22s"
Willow Review: "John Deere Green," "Miss Tuttle's Sixth Grade,
    Fulton Elementary," "Coming to Know My Fathers"
Wind: "The Farmer and the Silent *S*"
Worcester Review: "Explanations for the Night"
Yemassee: "On God's Tooth"

The following poems also appeared in the chapbook *Whatever
Was Ripe* (Bright Hill Press): "The Gleaners," "Farm Widow," and
"Merle Freeman's Auction."

About the Author

William Jolliff, professor of English at George Fox University, is a poet, critic, songwriter, and occasional banjo player. His previous books include *The Poetry of John Greenleaf Whittier: A Readers' Edition* (2000), *Heeding the Call: A Study of Denise Giardina's Fiction* (2020), and the poetry collection *Twisted Shapes of Light* (2015). He grew up on a farm just outside Magnetic Springs, Ohio, and now lives with his wife, Brenda, in Newberg, Oregon.